Knuckle Sandwiches

Knuckle Sandwiches

Tom Smario

Knuckle Sandwiches

Published by

🌾 Wheatland Press

http://www.wheatlandpress.com
P. O. Box 1818
Wilsonville, OR 97070

The Sweet Science, like an old rap
or the memory of love, follows its
victim everywhere. . .

A.J. Liebling

For Stephen Gordon,
brilliant ol' curmudgeon
of pugilistic affairs. . .

Introduction

I knew a boxer in New York City who once fought for the light heavyweight championship of the world--twenty years after the fact, he had gotten a little punchy. Whenever I didn't see him for a while, he'd forget about me; I'd just go out of his head. Then I would run into him again and he'd be all, Hey, man! Where you been?, as if suddenly he remembered me and couldn't understand why a couple of great friends like us weren't doing some serious hanging out. He was a sweet guy, good-hearted and well-meaning. Each time after I ran into him, he'd start showing up at my door at all hours, wanting to talk or get a beer, whatever, and eventually I'd have to push him away or else he'd move into my life full-time, something my life was too crowded to permit; but for a while we would hang out and talk and have that beer. Mostly we talked about boxing. He had fought during the seventies, when the light heavyweight division was populated by men like Matthew Saad Muhammad, Marvin Johnson, Victor Galindez, Yaqui Lopez, Dwight Muhhamad Qawi, Michael Spinks, Richie Kates, James Scott. Names that, for boxing people, are articles of faith, emblematic of courage and skill and toughness. It was the Golden Age of the division. I can't think of any weight division that had so much talent in it at once, and I liked hearing him talk about those days, those men.

One night we were sitting at the bar in the Westervelt Grill on Staten Island, and he zoned out for about fifteen, twenty minutes, something he was prone to do after a few drinks. He sat with his head down, nodding, whispering to himself. I drank and chatted up the bar maid. Finally he lifted his head and said, You know, if boxing was a country--and it is, kinda, y'know, like—the flag, man, it'd have this picture of a rattlesnake lying in some rocks and a motto that says, Be First.

This would have been a remarkable thing for anyone to have said in casual conversation, because it was a wonderful metaphor for the sport, for its violence and venemous politics; but to hear it proceed from the mouth of this poorly educated, brain-damaged man...it seemed that something—a spirit, a principle--was speaking through him. I wasn't altogether surprised to hear him say these words. Boxers are sometimes given to uttering oddly allusive and eloquent non-sequiters. But the point I'm attempting to make, somewhat circuitously, is that generally when people think about boxing, they think of two men fighting, they think how brutal and primitive it is, what an insult to the body it involves. I won't try to deny that prize fights are brutal and primitive. Those qualities are, to one degree or another, intrinsic to all competition, and fighting is competition in its purest form; but though the fight itself may lie at the heart of what compells many of us-- particularly journalists, artists, writers--to become passionate about boxing, it's the sport's blue collar exoticism that seals the deal. It's the stories that arise from it, the idiosyncratic traditions, the villains (and there are so many villains, the promoters who make their fighters' checks disappear; the commissions who license fighters with neurological deficits, unqualified ring doctors, incompetent referees and judges: rattlesnakes lying in the rocks) and the heroes and the cowards and the eccentric hangers on (as, for instance, Luis Sorea, an elderly Cubano who before every fight would taste Muhammad Ali's sweat to determine how strong he would be in the ring that night) and the obsessed trainers whose hearts are broken by a kid they've brought along since the age of fourteen and who leaves them for a promise of great things in which the kid should have known better than to believe. A fight is the culminative ritual of the sport, its communion feast; the litany and the doctrine and its true spirituality are hidden from public view, and that hidden part is where you hear the stories, meet the people, and engage all of boxing's romance and ugliness and truth.

If boxing were another planet, and it is, kind of—as unique in its gravities and physical obligations as is the earth--you would most effectively explore it not by sitting in front of a TV and watching two men fight, but by walking through the doors of a gym and, after a few years of exercising its disciplines and talking to its citizens, you would then understand something about the men fighting on TV, about why they're fighting (often a more complex reason than you might think) and what they actually win. One person you might want to talk to in this regard is Tom Smario, who's worked as a cornerman—a cutman, specifically—in rings all over the USA for the past several decades, who does not merely understand the sport, but breathes it, and, more pertinently, is so passionate about its stories, its romance, ugliness and truth, he's been driven to write two books of poetry about it, the second of which you hold in your hands.

Poetry may seem to you an incongruous complement to such a bloody sport, but if that's so, then your conception of poetry is badly skewed...and there are reasons for that. Back in the day, John Ciardi and Stephen Spender, poets who should have known better, used their influence and their platform (*The Saturday Review of Literature*) to channel American poetry into an effete and over-intellectualized pursuit. It gradually became the province of university professors, of men and women who perceived it as a rarefied act, one requiring a Classical education and a certain prissy, priggish temperament (though they might not have used those adjectives), who sat in rooms and thought about "the work" and poetics and contrived experiments in form. Poetry, to their minds, was something ill-suited for un-PhDed. By achieving this result, Spender and Ciardi cut poetry off from its roots, from the energy of experience—at least they narrowed the kind of experience that was deemed acceptable as a fit subject for poetry. They sought to limit poetry to the gray declensions of the upper middle class. Drunks like Li Po and villains like Francois Villon would not have been welcome to sit at the *Saturday Review* table. Occasionally someone would happen along--Bukowski, Dylan Thomas, some of the Beats--whose genius would force the poetry establishment to take notice of the furious energy they brought to the art, but the doyens of the establishment succeeded for the most part in delimiting the field. Having thus lost its power to connect with people other than those who ascribed to these conditions, poetry became increasingly unpopular until--disregarding of common concerns, removed from the rhythms of the street--it lost its audience and its subversive power.

Over the past twenty-five years, boxing has undergone a similar loss of audience and influence, this due to economic reasons that caused network television to drop it from their schedules, making it impossible for potential fans to follow the evolution of young fighters unless they buy Pay-Per-View and cable shows; and this is not the only similarity between the two disciplines. Both are refinements of the primitive, attempts to impose technique and structure upon basic urges, to channel energy into efficient and graceful forms of expression. At their best, they are simple and beautiful, unencumbered by unnecessary flourishes, and potent. When Francois Villon wrote, "...when I lie down at night/I have a great fear of falling..." he was throwing the poetic equivalent of a left hook to the heart. When Muhammad Ali, while leaping backward, knocked Cleveland Williams down with a left jab, he was Shakespeare delivering with apparent casualness one of those perfect opening lines—"Let me not to the marriage of true minds admit impediment..."--that stun you with their easy power. It's not, I think, a coincidence today that poetry has evolved into types of competition, word slams in bars and on national stages, and—in Japan--poetry boxing, an event in which two poets stand in a ring and recite. More significantly, the compression and creativity essential to becoming a great fighter, the precision of form and technique, is analogous to the demands of great poetry.

Every boxing arena and gym holds a bubble of air colored by the blood and science and irrationality of the fight game, and each of the poems in *Knuckle Sandwiches* constitutes a similar bubble whose air is steeped with the raw pungency of moments and events. Their specificity is a large part of their genius--no one else can tell you what Tom Smario is telling you here; no one else can illuminate this strange cultish sport and its relation to the universe in precisely the same accurate and unaffectedly evocative way; and the fact that he presents his poems with such deliberate craft and cleanness of line...Well, if I were to describe Tom Smario's poems, I would say that as a poet he's Marvin Hagler on a good night, working his right hook under to excellent advantage, coming steadily forward, breaking you down, and, if you give him half a chance--which you have done by opening his book--he is going to knock you out.

Lucius Shepard
Vancouver, Washington
May, 2004

Contents

All Things Being Equal

Observations of a Gym Rat

All Things Being Equal

My Career As a Pugilist

It was Friday Night
at the San Leandro Boys Club
1963 and I was looking good!
My jab was working, right hand
getting in, I even heard
my brother in the audience. I felt
like a white guy with Floyd Patterson
in my shoes. I was boxing a black kid
from Oakland named Lonnie. I had
Imagination. Lonnie had talent.

I remember waking up floating
on my back with radiant white light
blazing down on me with a silhouette
standing over me asking, "are you alright?"
I don't know if I'm knocked out
or if this is a near death experience
but I figured this must be the referee
because if it was God he wouldn't
have to ask.

Saga of 'The Kid'

The last time I saw
Johnny "The Kid" Jackson
he was boarding a plane
for Denver taking a six rounder
on short notice.

He was scheduled to fight
a skinny white guy with a so-so
record at 130 pounds
give or take a pound.
Jackson needed the money
so he jumps on a plane alone
and flies out of Portland
with his mind intact
and a ride waiting
at the airport.

Hardly a ride. An hour late
a '67 pick-up truck with a headlight out
and the driver tells Johnny
he's going to weigh in right now.
 "What!" The kid says, "it's 10:30
at night!" They go to a dirty Mexican
bar where the weigh-in is.
There's a scale on the dance floor
but the juke box is broken.
It's dark in there but he eyes
his opponent and makes weight.

He meets his Cornermen
and Cutman and continues to study
his opponent. No problem, he thinks
to himself, this guy is a punk.
Punk comes in two pounds under
making weight. He's lanky
with good muscle structure.
He steps off the scale and flexes.
His tendons look as strong
as the straps on an electric chair.

Fight time comes and the Cutman
wraps his hands and says "that'll be
fifty bucks." Then the Cornermen
each speak up and want five percent.
The inspector says "time to go"
and Johnny's in the ring bouncing
and riding the ropes, getting the feel
of the place. Then the opponent
climbs into the ring and it's NOT
the lanky white guy! It's a dark skinned
Mexican with tattoos and a scowl etched
on his face. The Kid screams
 "what the hell is this!"

Nobody's listening. "This isn't
the guy I'm suppose to fight!"
Then the bell rings and The Kid
and the Mexican are even straight up
for five hot rounds and The Kid's getting
his jab in and the right is finding

it's range and the Mexican is starting
to wheeze when suddenly the referee
steps in and says "okay, that's it"
and declares it a TKO for the Mexican.
 "What the hell is this, the fight is fixed too"
Jackson screams. Nobody heard him.
As soon as the fight was over the ring crew
was disassembling the ring and the officials
went home. The crowd didn't give a damn.
Nobody gave a damn.

The Kid got paid and bummed a ride
to the airport and headed back to Portland
with five hundred bucks in his pocket
and a sore nose the size of an apricot.
When he got off the plane at Alaska
Airlines, gate 16, the police were there
waiting for him where he was handcuffed
and arrested for parole violation.
Leaving the state.

Waiting For the Heavyweight Daddies

Crouched on the ring steps
blue corner, watching the big guys
two twenty plus, staring at one another
waiting for the bell to ring. The two
loneliest men in the world.

Imagine waiting to be bitten by
a large dog. What thoughts race out
of control? Is one scared the other
glad of it? Nerves like a tattered
rope holding wild horses tethered
to a broken fence post. Are they both
petrified of the first bell of the final
apocalypse? Do they have to pee?
Each has a mother somewhere who cannot
bear to watch. A mother who is praying.
Between the judge and the doctor,
the timekeeper sits like a footman
at the door of a war.

Armchair Intellectuals

They make me sick,
the armchair intellectuals
who sit on their asses
like dance critics who know
the ballet but never knew a dancer.
They watch boxing on television
with their swollen feet propped up
on diabetic coffee tables
taking notes and writing
articles about how sleazy
the Sweet Science is.

Don King is their favorite subject.
Don & Mike Tyson are the bloody bait
for the noble public to bite on.
Tyson can't help himself. He feeds
the media crackheads a high they
could never, never obtain in their
own lives. They ache for Mike.

Boxing is the woman they can't have.
She's a whore and they wanted a housewife.
So they pound their frustrated keyboards
stroke their mouse and bitchslap her
into articles published in magazines.
She's emotional, dangerous, beautiful,
she's the human comedy gone mad
at the expense of brave little men
from Aztec villages where widows
weep for dead Bantamweights.

Have they ever wiped the blood
off a man's face or felt frantically for a pulse
after he'd been knocked unconscious.
Do they realize the devastation of a bad
decision or the orgasm of victory.
Probably not. The bastards live in high rises
where HBO is free and computer hook-ups
out number residents. No pets, no children,
there isn't a typewriter or poet in the entire building.

Cutman

I've got three cuts
and two hands and the
God-damned doctor keeps
telling me to let him
look at them but it's
"what's that?" And "oops
sorry doc, I didn't hear ya"
and by then I've got the
bleeding stopped, the bell
rings, the ref screams and
I still get out late
because I'll be damned
if I'm gonna get out
before I put the finishing
touch on my work and
finalize it with Aquaphor
and a prayer.

Ring Canvas at the Grand Avenue Gym

Here's a canvas stretched taunt
24x24 framed by velvet ropes
like a Renaissance painting
of vast historical perspective.
It's a patchwork of splats
and blotches painted with
 the blood of hundreds of shades
of gladiators. It's been scuffed
by the shoes of countless artists,
 textured with salt, saliva & lougies.
There are grease spots where heads
crashed and egos deflated and stained
where they lay. There's drool and tears.
There are live organisms slithering across
the painted landscape from every
neighborhood in the city. It's a work
of art, it's a party. I've seen lesser pieces
in museums considered priceless.
Jackson Pollack step back!

All Things Being Equal

Discussing with a friend
the history of boxing
and the virtues of dignity
in warfare throughout the
twenties, thirties & forties,
when suddenly comes Hector
Camacho Jr. dressed like
a sheik riding a camel to
the ring and during the
introductions sashaying
around like a fairy
zigzagging down Castro St.,
San Francisco, dreaming
of Gorgeous George.

He has a worthy opponent
across the ring but the cameraman
is mesmerized by Jr.. This is
2001 I remind myself. The
cameraman probably has a hard-on.
The camel may be mechanical.
Maybe Hector isn't real but
something invented by networks
to boast ratings.

In the meantime I imagine
they have ESPN in heaven. I
imagine Jack Dempsey and
Henry Armstrong laughing like hell.
My friend, "The Bucket" faces
south and salutes Sonny Liston.
Hector continues to preen himself
like a parrot. All things being equal,
Gorgeous George would have
kicked his ass.

Club Fighters

I

There is something
about a man who gets his butt
whipped for very little money.
Month after month, small shows,
Indian Casinos, Las Vegas, they fill in
and make the shows go

Not Contenders but tough men
living on the edge that
need the hundred bucks
a round.

They get their brains
shook like a can of paint
in a mixer at the local
hardware store.

I like the losers. They work
real jobs and go to the gym
at night. They train between
diaper changes and lunch breaks
and when they make it to the gym
after work they're already tired
but they do, nevertheless, whatever
it takes. They need the money.

I like them because I know them
so well. You don't get to be a good
cutman working with winners.
Opponents are more at ease with
their situation and themselves.
They don't demand or complain
nor do they need their ego's fed
every five minutes. Often they
are actually tranquil before a
fight because the pressure is off
and less is expected.

The good ones, they know
how to lose and not get hurt.
They turn their heads with the
punches therefore minimizing
the impact. The skilled ones
can do that. The defensive
wizards can make it look
like they're getting their
clocks cleaned when really
they know how to turn
just so and parry.

Punches that would paralyze
the average Joe can be tricked
into nothing more than a gnat
kicking you in the big toe
or a horsefly punching you
in the nose.

II

Opponents are big business.
Supply and demand. A promoter
and matchmaker feed them like
a dealer feeds a junkie. Just
enough, make him want more.
Make him feel full yet keep
him hungry. Compliment him.

They take the punishment,
get paid, everybody's happy.
The rent's good for one more
month, the wife is too.
They take fights to pay bills,
groceries, to pay for soccer
for the kids who ask, "Daddy,
what happened?" when they
walk in the next morning after
a fight with their features
out of whack. What do you
tell a kid?

In the beginning they dreamed
the same fabulous dreams that
floated around the heads of
every champion before them.
The aspiration to become
somebody blossoms in the same
far fields where wildflowers
poke their heads up among
the blight of poverty to
make a garden.

III

EEG's don't lie. No sir.
You've either got brain
damage or you don't. It's
 a boxers best friend but he
doesn't know it. Like a friend
that takes the car keys from
his drunk buddy. I'll take
an EEG over the advice of an
old trainer or ex-wife that
wants the child support.
Trust me, and trust the EEG.

You see, I know so many
that quit too late. It's almost
always too late. Let's face it,
boxing is good for the soul,
but bad for the brain.

Nursing homes are full of them.
Tomato cans and club fighters.
Men who built the winning records
of the champions. Old boxers
remind me of old poets stumbling
out of neighborhood taverns talking
to themselves. Boxing is old.
Boxing is older than prostitution,
because before women started charging
men were fighting over them. Boxing,
my friend, is older than poetry.

For Adrian Kauffman

Better To Be Lucky Than Good

Who says boxing isn't immoral.
I mean, here we are, a group
of people who pay to sit around
a square canvas lagoon
surrounded by the traffickers
of Minority meat & Black fish,
feasting on our lust that leaves
us drooling like Pavlovs hounds.

The night Alexis Arguello
fought Aaron Pryor we bet
three hundred in counterfeit
fifty dollar bills, undetected
in a dark Latino bar full of
drunk Mexicans who got up
and paid us when the fight
was over. We bought beer
for everybody and got
the hell out of there.

Fear

I have prepared
and prayed with hundreds
of gladiators before battle
and I'll tell you, fear,
is like cocaine for all
of them. It makes their
reflexes razor sharp
and their minds
a prism of multi-tasks.
Fear is the high
they get and still
pass the drug test.
It's like having a mad
cat inside of you
clawing its way out.
I've helped fighters
in dressing rooms
going to executions
and I've helped the
executioner sharpen
the axe. I've wrapped
the hands of champions
and held the belt around
the arms of junkies
so tight their veins
begged for it. Ray Leonard
at his very best looked
like he was scared to death.
All of the opponents
of Marvin Hagler were.

A Gym Isn't Just A Gym

A gym isn't just a gym.
Most of the kids who come here
never make it to the pro's.
They come here to shadow box
in front of huge mirrors
and study themselves.
They skip rope, punch bags
spar and learn discipline
working hard. They listen
to wise old trainers who often
replace missing fathers. Men
who scold them when they need it.
Who knows what a young man
thinks about! The gym is an
asylum for the anarchy of raging
hormones. How different their
lives, how alike their hearts are.

Adventures in Women's Boxing

She came to the weigh-in
wearing a tight sweat suit
like a little pink pixie in pigtails.
She stepped on the scale
and the most they could coax
out of her was 99 pounds
and the contract said she needed
to weigh around 110. Commissioner
said "nope, come back tonight
and try again."

She eats a big breakfast, lunch,
lots of water, puts ankle weights
in her sports bra and fishing weights
in her socks, leaves her baggy shirt on
and weighs in again at 107 give
or take a pound pigtails and all.
The guy working the scale nods
and the show is on. Two hours later
fight time comes and I wrap her hands
and slip the gloves on. I notice she's
nervous. This is her first fight
and the other girls first fight also.

Bell rings and it's like watching
two squabs fight over a worm.
A peck, a punch, a puff of smoke
and the cynical public pays for it.
I have seen women that were
fantastic fighters. Women on par
with men except for punching power.
Lioness is more adept killer.
Lioness as vicious. Lucia Rijker
would whip everybody I work with.
In the meantime the two squabs
are still fighting but they haven't
hurt the worm yet.

Friday Night At The Lucky Eagle Casino

Quick & deliberate
I leap up the ring steps,
climb between the second
and third ropes, place a pancake
of coagulant carefully into the gash,
 apply exact pressure and let nature
take it's course.

Has he taken aspirin or eaten garlic?
Has he nicked vessels or showing bone?
The doctor and the referee are behind me
telling me to let them look at the cut.
Its long and under the eyebrow.
I act like I don't hear them.
(Just give me one shot at it, doc!)
I make them wait. I act the fool.
The referee is getting pissed.

Finally I let them see it. No blood!
Dry as a salami sandwich!
"God-damn" the ref says and
the doctor is speechless. My
fighter, Ron Pasek, may be
the toughest man on the planet
but it's not for his own good.
The ten second warning buzzer
sounds, I put something special
on the cut. The bell rings
and the man-eater across
the jungle leaps to the center
of the ring with his claws extended
like stilettos dipped in saliva & shit.
He has tasted blood and likes it.

For Katherine Dunn

If Emily Dickinson Met Mike Tyson

Emily Dickinson would have
sliced Iron Mike into
short stubby stanzas

dressed him in flowers,
bad attitude, tragedy,
comedy

she would add
"a dash of pink
a dab of purple"

countless butterflies
blue birds, rose & lily.
Emily would destroy
the myth of Mike she would
bring out the feminine side
cuddle him, make him cry.

"You little shit" she would
say, "bring me the newspaper!"
and Mike would & Emily would

pen something sweet something
soft about her new
puppy.

Thoughts From the Red Corner

Crouched in the red corner waiting
for the bell to ring so I can go to work
on my man who is losing. Eyebrow cut,
bloody nose. My hand trembles momentarily
then I get a hold of myself. The future
is in my fingertips applying pressure.
I kiss the wounds and pray for a miracle.
I listen to the crowd, the comedy gone mad,
each player is screaming wildly, intoxicated
with advice, criticism, crap from the ringside seats,
crapola from the cheap seats. I listen
to the rude voices singing trinkets
of illiterate dumbbell babble. Come on,
come on I think to myself! Come all
you philosophers, bullshit artists
and so called boxing experts. Come all
you writers, journalists and painters
spreading it around colorful. Come all
you armchair trainers, imaginary cutmen,
cornermen in waiting. Come all
you chickenshits hallucinating yourself
up there in the big bad ring. Come all
you women looking doe-eyed
sitting in the first few rows wearing
fake faces and cheap hair. Come all
you fat-cats sitting next to them with
wives and kids at home. Come all
you mindless middle-aged drones
squeezing your little nuts between your weak thighs.

Come all
you tough guys, beer bellies,
hair growing out of ears. Come all
you Slick Willies wearing a wet spot
and bright white shoes. Come all
you businessmen. Come all
drunk jackasses shouting
obscenities with full bladders. Come all
you gutter balls, goof balls, bull balls
and foul balls with foul mouths. Come all
you drunk poets who probably had to sneak in.
Come kiss my ass, kiss my fighters ass!
Kiss it twice! Ladies and gentlemen
I love boxing. I've always loved boxing.

El Toro Salvaje Del Barrio

The jungle lying dormant
in most of us grows wild in Ruben Torres.
It's mystery, it's reptile thoughts
and killer cats stretch like tendons
from Yacatan to Oregon and work muscles
of heartbeats and survival instinct.
Charles Darwin would have given him
his own classification. Placed him
somewhere between man and bull
betraying his theory of evolution.
Ruben didn't evolve, he appeared
one day at the Grand Avenue Gym,
put on some boxing gloves
and proceeded to hit guys so hard
their fillings fell out of their mouths.
He has a six inch scar from a bullet
and eyes as soft as the underbelly
of love. He adores his mother.
He ate the guy that shot him.

I Know A Greater Fighter When I See One

The first time I saw
Michael Spinks I was driving
up Broadway in Portland
where I parked my van
in the middle lane,
ran across the street
and shook his hand.
Horns were honking
people were yelling at me
to move. I didn't give a damn.

The Friday Night Fights

A hot California night
thick with mystery and me,
teenage & senseless
sitting alone in a dark room
watching a beer commercial
in black and white. Then
the fight started. Ruben
"Hurricane" Carter came out
of his corner with demonic eyes
and a scyth. Emile Griffith
pirouetted out of his, graceful
as a dancer. Emile was a
Friday Night Fight regular.
Carter scared white people.
They may have been the two
most beautifully built men
who ever fought. Suddenly Carter
starts throwing bombs and
Emile is kissing them. Then
a left that would drop the
Statue of Liberty. Emile went
down hard and his eyes
were like two foxholes
with dead soldiers inside.

Teamwork In The Blue Corner

The Seconds can make a fighter
look better than he is. A make-up man
talks a blue streak and beautifies
a beaten fighters body language.
"Poetry, I want poetry!" The Second screams.
Another one pours ice water down his trunks.
All history is proof that ice water
on a man's nuts will wake him up.
The Cutman gives him a rinse,
then a drink from the Fountain Of Hope.
Vaseline. (don't get it on the eyelashes)
Then advice in a calm voice. And Daddy.
Daddy's the manager. Daddy don't do shit.

Fight Posters

The walls of the Grand
Avenue Gym are plastered
with them. They patch holes
and replace paint.
Like war memorials
these walls tell the history
of men and conquests
and the society they
lived in. They go back
to "colored boys," "wops"
and "white hopes" but
now we're politically correct
without adjectives.

People stare at them
and say "oh, remember him,
remember that fight? What
a fight!" Folks, if old posters
could talk they would stutter
like old prize fighters and tell
stories about winning, money
and glory. They wouldn't mention
the ghosts of the dead brain cells
that haunt the empty spaces
where memory was.
They forget about the hearts
broken by the reality of pugilism
that decapitated so many dreams.
Old fight posters are full
of young faces. Faces like
hopeful revolutionaries willing
to die for a cause. Faces with
noses as crooked as Michelangelo's.
Veterans of glorious wars.
This wall!

Joe Frazier & Ali's First Fight

Muhammad held the hook
baited with Smokin' Joe Frazier
dangled in front of white America

did his magic, sharpened his knives,
split his tongue and cackled
like a Magpie.

Suddenly Joe's the white man's white hope
Joe, blacker than the ink journalists
used to paint him white with.

Joe picked the cotton
used to make the clothes
for a middle-class Cassius.

1971. The white man was scared
of the black man. Writers and intellectuals
fought to fondle the Emperors new clothes.

The nation on a guilt trip
believed Joe Frazier was us
and we had it coming.

Observations of a Gym Rat

Observations Of A Gym Rat

The spit bucket,
a cioppino of racial genetics
contains about six inches
of saliva, old strands
of tape and hand wraps,
bloody boogers and lougies
that float like little boats.
It sits by the ring steps,
a garlicky stew of humanity
purged into a silver chalice.

The tall mirrors
on the walls create illusions.
I've seen kids, professionals
and hardened criminals shadowboxing
in front of them. Each sees whatever
they choose. I look at myself,
laughter ensues. I know
lady novelists that work out
in front of them and loose themselves
and poets that loose their minds.
I've watched young men study themselves
and aging gladiators in denial.
I've watched wannabe's and champions
next to contenders and tomato cans
with imagination. I once fought

Sugar Ray Robinson in front
of a ten foot mirror. It was a hell
of a fight. I knocked Sugar Ray out
in the sixth round.

The tired towel hanging
from the ring's turnbuckle
is tie-dyed with blood
oil and salty sweat.
Hundreds of bloody noses
have gushed and ripped
lips painted it colorful.

This pastiche of pain
hangs limp and lifeless
like evidence at a crime scene.

The heavy bag
hangs like a dead hog,
black and bloated
swinging from a beam.

The speed bag
is more temperamental.
It's got to be
in the mood to sing.

The music the rope makes
makes me want to dance.
The lyrics of the song
are pure poetry.

One guy I know
brings this huge rottweiler
into the gym and parks him
right next to the ring.
He pets the dog
and the dog licks him.
Then he asks people
if they want to spar with him.
I look at him and ask,
"are you crazy?"

The University of Pain

The smell is the first thing
that hits you. It's a frying pan
in the face, a fire in the nostrils.
It's forbidding and beautiful
the smell of men training to
maim one another. The essence
of every neighborhood in the city.
The gym is a miniature cosmos
without ventilation.

Then the music. The songs
of the rope, the heavy bags
like bass drums, the rhythm
of the speed bag sounds like
a rattlesnake shaking it's tail.
The pro's, music to them
are happy dollars singing
in their wallets. Who can
blame them?

The University Of Pain
is where the students
and professors congregate.
If you want to be a prize fighter
you have to pay your dues,
work hard, keep your mouth
shut and listen. You have to
take notes and hope your blood
doesn't delude your memory.

In the ring, men spar and learn
their craft from grizzled old men
who are trainers. They used to
be fighters. This is where young men
come to sharpen their knives.
They learn to shoot and duck,
shuck and jive with destiny.
Some get good and some don't.
In the gym they don't give grades.
You either get respect or you don't.

The Great Thumbers

I love the great thumbers.
The ones who think like Picasso
or a cross-eyed architect using
angles and imagination. Who
can forget the precision thumb
of Roberto Duran incapacitating
Davey Moore. Remember the big
thumbs of Larry Holmes who
thumbed everybody but the Pope.
Larry was a maestro. And Eusebio
Pedroza who would have poked
Mickey Mouse in the eye after
he hit him low. They say that
Fritzie Zivic had great thumbs
but I don't know. I wasn't born
yet, but if it's the thumbs he used
on Henry Armstrong, he's a dirty
sonofabitch.

The Trainer & The Teacher

He was a wizened old Mexican
that stood ten feet tall
among the Latino boxers
that gathered in the corner
we called "Little Tijuana."

Jesse Sandoval, God plucked
him from his garden and transplanted
him in the Grand Avenue Gym.

He taught his "kids" how to knock
a man out and respect and love
mankind at the same time.

Jack Dempsey In Four Wheel Drive

He jumps a plane
from Canada, goes wherever
the plane lands, shows up
shuts up and keeps winning.

License current, passed
the drug test, Georgino the promoter
can't ask for any more than that.

Bell rings and Ron Pasek
hustles like a trachoe eating
mounds of meat, tearing flesh
from bone, like Jack Dempsey
in four wheel drive.

Lucky Eagle Casino, sometime
in 2001 in front of 1200 drunk
screaming people.

He comes back to the corner,
I take the mouthpiece out, clean
him off and look at the poor guy
he just knocked out. I help him
put his robe on, cut the hand wraps
off and give him a drink. The referee
raises his hand and he hugs the loser.
Believe it or not, he even pays
his cornermen.

The Boxing Coach

He walked into
the neighborhood gym
with a chip
on one shoulder
and a vulture
on the other
and tattoos
like graffiti
on the walls
of hell.

Twenty-four years
and a career later
he's still here
coaching kids like
himself, fixing chips
and turning heads,
mesmerizing boys
with wisdom and whip.
"Where's your report cards,
let me see your report cards
or nobody works out!"

Human Nature & The Battling Buddhist

I feel that there are
inherent qualities in men & women
that sing out at pugilistic affairs.
War, ignorance and violence pursed
on the lips of the devil whistling
some patriotic tune.
Take for example the drunk jackass
screaming over and over "break his arm off
and beat his ass with it!" He's sitting
two seats from the blue corner
and spills beer on the floor.
His old baseball hat says
"Vietnam Veteran" and sits cocked
on his lopsided grey-haired head.
A patch on his jacket says "I'll Forgive
Jane Fonda When The Jews Forgive Hitler"
I don't get the connection, but then
I never went to Vietnam and I never
met Hitler. The guy won't shut up.
It's like a jackhammer on my heart
or a chopstick in my ear and my fighter
who is from Cambodia is getting
his ass kicked by a Mexican kid.
"Break his arm off and beat his ass with it"
Sinan Kuch, "The Battling Buddhist", catching hell,
comes back to the corner. I pour ice water
on his head, down his pants, give him
a drink and put some Vaseline on his face.
The jackass behind me is still braying.
Bell rings and Sinan, who doesn't hear
a thing bounces out of his corner

ready to battle. Racism is a natural thing.
Like the dragon on the back of Sinan's
green silk robe, it sits at ringside
and it's tongue comes out of it's mouth
and licks itself into a frenzy.

The Great Mark "Too Sharp" Johnson

At the weigh-in
my guy comes in real heavy.
He's tired, traveled from Mexico,
half-starved fighting in a strange city.
Mark and me and the commissioner
go outside and Mark says "listen,
let the weight go the way it is. It's okay.
I know what the guy's going through."
Commissioner says fine, I say thanks,
shake hands and look at him. No
bigger than a Idaho potato
he had class. Poised as a panther,
eyes focused, intense concentration
he had better balance than Segovia's
fingers strumming some smooth song.
Fight time comes and "Too Sharp"
mesmerizes Mexico leading him
around the ring and punishing him
ever so nicely. I tore my pants
before the fight in the dressing room
working the mitts with Mexico,
and worked his corner
in my underwear.

Fight Of The Year

Working out at the New Oakland
Boxing Gym, Andy Heilman was doing
sit-ups. "Forty-four, forty-five
forty-six" his trainer holding his
feet was calling out the numbers.
A guy in the corner named Snakebite
was cracking jokes on the heavy bag
which wasn't laughing. Dick Sadler
was talking to a fifteen year old kid
who wouldn't leave him alone while he
watched Charlie Shipes hit the speed
bag. Charlie was pure class. Hugging
the heavy bag, Freddie Root was laughing
at something Nate Collins said. Across
the bay, in San Francisco, Jimmy Lester
was becoming more vicious than ever.

The Oakland Auditorium reeked with cigar
smoke mixed with farts and the body odors
of various cultures sitting side-by-side
not by choice but by seat number. So many
of the greats fought there their souls
linger in the dressing rooms and shadow
box in the hallways. In the cheap seats
were kids like myself, delirious with
magic, crazy with dreams and jacked up
on adrenalin. "In this corner, from Fargo,
North Dakota, is Andy Heilman, Heilman!"

The ring announcer bawled. My brother
and father clapped and were lost in the
ovation. "And in this corner, from Hunter's
Point, San Francisco is Jimmy Lester, Lester!"
And the crowd roared and screamed and I screamed
along with them.

Heilman, a cowboy had fought bulls
in taverns across the Northwest and Plains.
Heilman fought in places so lonely nobody
saw the fight. He had the body language
of a sonofabitch and the muscle structure
of stubborn men who worked sun-up to sundown
bailing hay. Not showy, mind you, but strong.
Jimmy Lester was born for it. Strictly
carnivorous, a predator he could actually
summon the rage of the ghetto and channel
it into the fury of his fists. The chemistry
of his disposition sustained blazing electrons
of anger. Jimmy Lester was the definition of
a bad motherfucker

The first canto exploded like a race riot.
Any fight between a Black man and a White man
can. Both guys brought their armies along with
the artillery of muscle and emotion. Sportsmanship
was abandoned. You could hear cannons going off
and ribs crying out in agony. Only the timekeeper
was in control. Both men became demented with
the orgasmic intensity of the moment. Scuffles

broke out in the crowd. The entire place became
 one big fight. Everybody hit somebody and some
people slugged themselves. Heilman threw punches
like a claustrophobic madman with a baseball bat.
Lester fought like Lester was. A man swinging
an axe in wide arcs and roundhouses that tear
meat from the bone.

For ten rounds or ten years or all the time
in the world they could not come to terms.
The judges called it a draw. A wise move.
Regardless of the strategy plotted before the
bout or in the minute between rounds they
remained locked in a bloody street brawl
held with cables covered with soft green
velvet. A civil war among people sanctioned
by the state. They were not two men, two
boxers, they were generations of men with
a history of lousy relations that hated
each other for whatever reasons. Now Lester,
now Heilman tried to kill the other. Damn
sure did. Neither won or lost, nor were
they ever the same men again.

Dance Class For Gladiators

I have seen the finest
dancers on the planet
in the gym, gliding across
the ring like ghosts
on a Ouija Board
without gravity, ducking
punches, juking destiny.

Willie Pep, Ray Leonard
this is where they learned to dance
and a million kids with young legs.
In the gym, dance class
is for gladiators and if you
don't pass you get punched.

Fighting In New Orleans

Sweating on a white iron bench
in the French Quarter waiting
for Ricardo Medina, Bantamweight
Champion who is getting his palm
read by an ugly old Creole fortune
teller who tells him that a spell
has been cast on him by a past
lover and he's not "clean" and has
to get "clean" because his destiny
depends on it and she doesn't "clean"
anybody until after 6 o'clock and I'm
sitting there like a gargoyle that needs
a cold beer & Richard "Casanova" the
manager, we're both thinking, oh for
Christ's sake don't tell him that,
"clean" him now! Clean him now!
She says a very powerful Brujo in
Mexico City has cast this spell and
she cannot do it until sunset and I'm
thinking to myself, listen lady he
fights in a few hours, we don't need
any spells because our opponent is
already ten years younger and
undefeated and Ricardo is defending
his title & believes in witch doctors,
believes in Brujos and witchcraft.

Ricardo believes and if we wait
until sunset we'll hit rush hour
traffic and miss the fight, clean or dirty
we won't make it as flies buzz,
jazz drifts & the ghosts of voodoo mommas
circle above us sweat runs down the angelic
face of the Virgin Of Guadalupe tattooed
on his brown back.

Immigrant Heart

Walking from the dressing room
to the ring with Lightweight
Juan Roman there were no
musicians to lead us. No
cameras, feathered Aztec dancers
or friends from Acapulco
waving flags. Just Leonard,
Molly & me. Lucky Eagle Casino.
Juan bounced around, felt the ropes
and speed of the canvas. The
announcer botched his name.
Bell rings. He advanced by feet,
retreated by inches. An immigrants'
heart! Teeth. Claws. Punches like
a two headed snake. A spirit
willing to die. There have been
Mexican fighters more decorated
but there are no Mexican
wolverines as mean.

The Saturday Afternoon War

It was like sitting on
a hillside having a picnic
during the Civil War
watching the oscillating
cannon fire of two gun ships
gone mad.

One Black, one Indian.
A television commercial
every third round.
Something for everybody.
Dazzling combinations,
bad intentions & heart.
An ebb of action slapping
the spectators in the ass.

Mathew Saad Muhammad!
Abandoned on destiny's doorstep.
Champion! Yaqui Lopez was
the bravest warrior that never
wore a crown.

Confession Of A Judas Goat

They come from
small towns without
trainers or cornermen
to fight the "house" fighters.

They take buses, pass
the physical, drug test
and eye exam which
makes them qualified.
Nameless, without God
given talent, promoters
ask me to work their corners.
I feel like a Judas goat
leading a lamb to slaughter.

The entertainment of boxing
needs players. I lead them
without a leash to where
the executioner waits.
The announcer gives
the crowd some irrelevant
information about them
and often pronounce
their name wrong.

Then the act.
Headless, I guide them
out of the ring, back to the bus.
They got paid, promoter's happy.
Fans could care less. It's
all about money.

Defense As Art

Roy Jones floated
like a song
over a dance floor
controlling the tempo.

Ego, combinations,
dazzling right hands,
left hooks, ego.

I sat next to the ring
and watched an Englishman
put intense pressure
on him. Backed him up.

He worked and wiggled
and eased off the ropes
and looked down a blouse
at ringside.

Rafael From Reno

Bell rings to end
the ninth round
and Rafael, from Reno
comes back to the corner
and sits down like a man
waiting for a lazy train.
I got into his face and
made eye contact and calmly
told him he needed
a knockout to win.
Then I showed him
a photograph of his
three kids I borrowed
from his wallet.

Bell rings again.
Rafael swaggers forward,
drunk-like and throws
a round right hand
that lands like a sock
full of rocks. The other guy
goes down and never sees
the end of the round.

Tribute To The Last Great Generation

Fourteen days ago
my brother told me,
if you don't get here
within 48 hours I don't think
you'll ever see our father again.

What miracle made
Archie Moore get up
against Yvonne Durell?
What kept Tony Zale upright?
What quality? Picture Henry Armstrong
fighting once a week riding
hungry boxcars to his fights.
My father was a Ball Turret Gunner!
He loved Willie Pep, Max Baer
and Kid Gavilan. Joe Louis
eclipsed the conscience
of a racist society. Joe was
the go-ahead for Great America.

Today my father and I
went out to breakfast, two weeks later.
From Armstrong to Rocky Graziano
The Depression left an impression.
If you count, they'll probably get up.

Mercy

End of the fourth terrible round
in Santa Cruz fighting
future champ Shane Mosley
and Jose Luis Madrid
from Tijuana, has a look
on his face like a soldier
in shock.

I give him a small swig
of California agua. Nothing
fancy, I go it out of the tap.
"I can't take anymore"
he says to me and Richard
"Casanova" and "Casanova"
the manager who wants to cry
says, "I don't blame you."

Waiting

Sitting in room 4183
Wyndham Anatole Hotel
Dallas, Texas with Ricardo Medina
watching Univision on t.v.
which I do not understand.
Ricardo tries to translate
but he doesn't speak English.
My tongue in Spanish moves
as clumsy as a Gila Monster.
Our hearts speak the same
language. Downstairs in the
Grand Ballroom that truly is,
1500 seats are sold out at a
thousand bucks a pop. Bankers,
real estate moguls and politicians
will squeeze their wealthy rumps
next to wives and women
more elegant than money. Between
the prelims and the main event
they are raffling off a half dozen
Harley Davidson motorcycles.
They tell me every other seat
will contain a millionaire. Win
or lose, Ricardo will head back
to a poor neighborhood in Mazatlan
and I'll head back to Portland.
Tonight he fights Gilberto Corrales
for the North American Bantamweight
Championship. Corrales is 19-0
with 16 knockouts. Handsome as hell.
The line says Ricardo is a 3-1 underdog.

We on the other hand, if we pooled
our money together couldn't afford
a ticket to our own fight. Ricardo
prays with a rosary with broken beads.
I'm eating light because I need to
save the food money. I'd love a
beer. No, a couple of beers.

A Boy's Dream

I wanted to be a boxer.
All boys of my generation
aspired to have the ability
of Muhammad Ali. Not me!
I wanted Marvin Hagler's
fury and steel. I'm 5'3".
I wanted to chop down
the biggest tree
on the playground.

Fundamentals

Working the mitts
with a young Mexican
named Gabrial who
listens to me better
than my kids did.

He's got the eyes.
Attentive, focused, a bit
of Zen. He's so fast,
when he shadow boxes
the shadows can't keep up.

Speed is power. He singes
the mitts punching holes
through imaginary opponents.
We practice combinations,
angles, theory & principal.
We practice trickery.

To break a man down
takes ambition. You need
an architect, a plan
and some poor sucker
crazy enough to get
into a ring with this kid.

The Death Of Boxing In America

We've evolved.
It's to tame. We'd rather
bomb Brown people
than watch them box.

The artistry of Muhammad Ali
has been replaced by
Shock & Awe.
Smart bombs better
educated than the people
who use them.

Boxing as violence
isn't interesting enough.
It's not spectacular.
Media is GOD!
Boxing bows to the
malfunction of America.

Acknowledgements

I would like to thank the editors of The Cyber Boxing Zone, www.cyberboxingzone.com, where the following poems first appeared: Cutman, All Things Being Equal, My Career As A Pugilist, Joe Frazier & Ali's First Fight and Waiting For The Heavyweight Daddies.

The poems, Ring Canvas At The Grand Avenue Gym, Fight Posters, Observations Of A Gym Rat, The University of Pain, The Trainer & The Teacher, The Boxing Coach and Dance Class For Gladiators appeared in the book, "Fighters: The Quest For Glory And The Struggle for Survival In America's Toughest Boxing Gyms."

Waiting For The Heavyweight Daddies also appeared in The North American Boxing Federation newsletter.

Fight Of the Year first appeared in NOTES OF A CORNERMAN, Peninhand Press, Portland, Oregon 2000.

I would also like to thank Babe Smario for blessing me with the spirit, and Marilyn Smario for being the catalyst for the fires that burn the boundaries down. Thanks to Katherine Dunn for years of friendship and encouragement. Additional thanks to Lucius Shepard and Eric Jorgensen for the thumbs up.

Finally, I would like to thank Mike Thomsen and Fred Ryan for having enough faith to believe in lost causes.

Photography and cover photo by Jim Lommasson.

Tom Smario
May, 2004

Other books by Tom Smario

THE SOLES OF MY SHOES (1975)

LINES (1978)

LUCKYNUTS & REAL PEOPLE (1979)

THE CAT'S PAJAMAS (1982)

SPRING FEVER (1985)

NOTES OF A CORNERMAN (2000)

www.ingramcontent.com/pod-product-compliance
Lightning Source LLC
LaVergne TN
LVHW091207080426
835509LV00006B/868